A *Seth Eastman* SKETCHBOOK

ACKNOWLEDGMENT

THE PUBLISHERS ARE GRATEFUL TO THE PEARL BREWING COMPANY FOR PERMISSION TO REPRODUCE IN THIS VOLUME THE DRAWINGS CONTAINED IN SETH EASTMAN'S SKETCHBOOK. THE SKETCHBOOK ITSELF HAS RECENTLY BEEN PRESENTED BY THE PEARL BREWING COMPANY TO THE MARION KOOGLER MCNAY ART INSTITUTE FOR ITS PERMANENT COLLECTION.

A SETH EASTMAN

SKETCHBOOK, 1848-1849.

INTRODUCTION BY LOIS BURKHALTER

Published for the Marion Koogler McNay Art Institute,
San Antonio, by the University of Texas Press, Austin

CONTENTS

Introduction

A SMALL BOOK OF DRAWINGS—a priceless record of Texas and the Lower Mississippi River made over a century ago —has been presented to the Marion Koogler McNay Art Institute by the Pearl Brewing Company of San Antonio.

This pictorial record, of major importance to art as well as to history, is contained in a modest leather-bound sketchbook, the kind that fits neatly in the pocket of a soldier on the move. On the cover the owner burned his name: *Seth Eastman*.

Fortunately, it found its way back to San Antonio, where Captain Eastman, U. S. Army, did some of his finest drawings and paintings. That the Eastman Sketchbook remains permanently in San Antonio is due largely to Paul Adams, a San Antonio businessman and history enthusiast, who recognized its value to Texas when it was offered for sale in 1947 by Eastman's great-granddaughter, Mrs. Anna Jayne Moebs. Mrs. Moebs received it from her mother, daughter of Commodore Thomas Henderson Eastman, U. S. Navy, the artist's oldest son.

Mr. Adams interested the Pearl Brewing Company in purchasing the

Sketchbook. Later, through a most happy incident, he acquired a companion piece, a journal kept by Eastman on the same Texas tour of duty, which is still in his possession.

In January, 1960, the Sketchbook was publicly shown for the first time at the McNay Art Institute, where it has found a permanent home.

The two documents fill a gap in Eastman's scanty biographical material. Formerly the only information available on Eastman's Texas tour was contained in brief Army records and a few letters in the Sibley Papers of the Minnesota Historical Society. Even so, much is still unknown and unrecorded. Although a prolific sketcher, Eastman was sparse of words and shy of pen. His memoirs are laconic and scattered. Eastman's most resourceful biographer, John Francis McDermott, has written the first full-length study of the artist, which will be published in October by the University of Oklahoma Press.

Eastman, born in Brunswick, Maine, in 1808, graduated from the United States Military Academy in 1829, and was assigned to the First Infantry. He was forty years old when ordered to Texas to aid in protecting the frontier against marauding Indians and in establishing a line of frontier forts.

Texas was not his choice of assignments.

The appointment he wanted, and for which he applied, was that of illustrator for a mammoth report on Indians authorized by Congress the year before and being prepared by Henry Rowe Schoolcraft, an Indian agent. But the War Department, too intent at the moment on exterminating the Indian to be mindful of recording him for posterity, sent Eastman to Texas, where the Comanches were blocking the state's westward expansion.

In that year, 1848, the United States, for the first time since Texas was annexed, found time to give a close look to the sparsely settled state. The treaty with Mexico required an official survey of the boundary. Emigrants to the west were urged to take the Texas route, but there were no established roads to follow and travelers as well as Texans demanded the protection of the United States Army.

Eastman was one of a great number of soldiers, scouts, surveyors, and engineers assigned to Texas. His tour of duty at the time made small impression on the big state. His presence was not recorded by contemporary journalists although his reputation as an artist even then was considerable. He was still better known as an Indian fighter. During the past nineteen years he had participated in numerous full-scale operations against the Sioux and Winnebagoes at Fort Crawford, Wisconsin, and Fort Snelling in Minnesota, and against the Seminoles in Florida.

In September, 1848, Eastman left Fort Snelling, where he had spent a great part of his Army life, and started down the Mississippi River, pencil and sketchbook in hand. The Captain's meticulous care in keeping his pencils sharpened to the finest point is one reason his drawings remain distinct and clean after more than a century.

Eastman left his art career in the capable hands of his wife, Mary, and his influential friend, Henry S. Sibley, delegate to Congress from Minnesota. His absence in the interior of Texas would remove him from the sphere in which he was beginning to be recognized as the foremost Indian painter of his day. Fort Snelling, although an outpost, was one of the most visited places on the western front.

There he had met and become friends with a number of visiting journalists and artists who were impressed by Eastman and his Indian paintings. From Fort Snelling he could keep in touch with the National Academy of Design, of which he was an "honorary member amateur," and the American Art Union, which that year had purchased six of his paintings.

Eastman possessed the skill of drawing in the smallest possible space and a trained eye for the minutest detail, qualifications needed in the type of delineation developed at West Point for topographical engineers who were to give the world the first authentic views of the unknown West.

He had been assigned to topographical duty in 1831 and later was assistant teacher of drawing at the United States Military Academy when the noted artist, Robert W. Weir, was training cadets destined to chart and depict the American West. Eastman's *Treatise on Topographical Drawing*, published in 1837, was used as a textbook at West Point.

The Upper River was well known to Eastman. At one time he had proposed publishing a picture book of it. Some of his views of this section made on the 1848 tour are in the collections of the Peabody Museum of Archaeology and Ethnology and of the Minneapolis Public Library.

Doubtless, as he recorded the River, he considered making a panorama, a type of travelogue then popular. Less talented artists had found it lucrative. But unlike them, Eastman preferred the less spectacular scenes, and bypassed many places already made familiar by repetition.

The Mississippi River views in the Sketchbook begin fourteen miles above Sainte Genevieve on the Missouri bank and end at the Southwest Pass below New Orleans.

Eastman's River is serenely placid, often desolate and gloomy, and always lovely and remote. The sandbars and towheads, the bends and cut-offs, the snags and sawyers and driftwood, the hulks of wrecked boats—these and all the other perils which beset the river pilots—Eastman saw, not as threats to life and boat, but as objects unobtrusively placed to avoid monotony.

Eastman turned his attention from the passing scene to portray an unidentified steamboat pilot at the wheel in the pilot's house. Above Cairo he drew the tree-covered hills, rock precipices, and old French settlements. At the Ohio River junction he was attracted by the variety of craft—pirogues, flatboats, keelboats, a ferry, and a wharf boat. Inside the wharf boat he sketched a group of men waiting.

Passing between Arkansas and Tennessee he pictured the wood yards and stumpy banks, log cabins and rail fences, cotton plantations, slave quarters, and villages. His views of Vicksburg are among the most charming in the book. Two-story houses hug the waterfront and sit on the terraces above; the bakery and grocery store rise impressive structures resembling fortresses.

Near the end of his long river ride he sketched the sugar plantations on the low Louisiana bank. Eastman's drawings of New Orleans were made from the tower of Jackson Barracks, a few miles from present-day Jackson Square. The profile of the town from that distance is on a microscopic scale, but nevertheless it is recognizable and the landmarks are discernible.

At this point he recorded his mileage: "1040 miles below the Ohio, 2044 from Pittsburg, 1212 from St. Louis, 105 from the Balize, 17 from Fort St. Leon, 73 from Fort St. Phillips, 1944 from Fort Snelling."

Since Eastman passed that way the Mississippi has changed its course many times, and some of his River towns are no longer on the River. Floods and time have erased others and only Eastman's drawings remain to tell us how some of them looked.

His last sketches of the Mississippi, which he left on October 31, are of the pilot houses at the mouth and the sailboats and steamers at the South-west Pass.

Eastman's first glimpse of Texas revealed a row of small pilot houses, hardly substantial enough to withstand a breeze, on the flat and treeless north beach of Matagorda Bay. The houses at the entrance to the bay indicate a recent blow—one is atilt in the water. Eastman explains this on a map of the area where he marked an "X" to designate a wreck and noted: "arrived in Matagorda Bay on 5th Nov. 48, day after the danger of being wrecked."

As he approached Indian Point (Indianola), his port of entry, he sketched two views of it. Ten days later Eastman and his company were on the march, taking the road to Seguin. Along the way he drew the native trees —moss-draped post oaks, groves of ancient live oaks, and mesquites, which he was perhaps seeing for the first time. Seguin was a small cluster of cabins in a forest of oaks. Eastman singled out one of architectural significance— two rooms, made of logs, with a dog-run between.

Eastman began his group of San Antonio drawings, the most authoritative and detailed ones known, at Mission San José, shown with its original façade, carved doors, statuary, dome, and tower. Later he returned to sketch the cloister arches. (In the Peabody Museum is also a pencil sketch of the Mission's granary.)

The Sketchbook contains four views of the ruins of the Alamo, as it looked twelve years after the Revolution, shortly before its roof was replaced and the structure was used as an Army quartermaster's depot. At the Watch Tower, two miles from the Alamo, Eastman made a telescopic profile of the town, dominated by the towers of old San Fernando Church. On his return from Fredericksburg the following March he did a close-up of the church, hemmed in by adobe structures, fronting the plaza.

Other Eastman pencil and watercolor drawings of the Alamo, the Watch Tower, San Fernando, and Missions Concepción and San Juan are in private and museum collections.

Early in December Eastman and his soldiers started into the "Comanche" country of scrubby hills and clear creeks to take command of a frontier post near Fredericksburg, which at that time was known as "Camp Houston." Shortly thereafter it was named "Fort Martin Scott," in honor of an officer by that name who was killed in the war with Mexico.

Fredericksburg had been established only two years before, deep in the Comanche country, where only the colonists of the Society for the Protection of German Immigrants in Texas dared to venture.

Eastman's first drawing of the Hill Country is labeled "20 miles North of San Antonio Texas Dec. 2, 1848 looking South" and "5 miles north of Baron Misinburg."

Eastman referred to Baron John O. von Meusebach, who had retired the year before as commissioner general of the German Society and was farming at Comanche Springs in Bexar County. It is possible that Eastman called on Meusebach, whose fame was considerable and who probably knew the Comanche better than any other man in Texas. After founding Fredericksburg and depositing 120 settlers in a section of Texas considered extremely hazardous, Meusebach penetrated even deeper into Indian territory to find the Comanches and make a peace treaty between them and the German settlers.

As an artist, Eastman was primarily concerned with Indian life. Yet in Texas the trees, the hills, and the structures held his interest, the Indian appearing only occasionally as a faint figure in the background. At Camp Houston he must have been in daily contact with the Indians who came to trade with the Germans, but as a subject he selected the life of the German colonist. His Fredericksburg drawings are a priceless record of the early-day German architecture. Less than two years old at that time, the structures appear as ancient survivors of another era.

Among them is an extremely rare item, the "Dutch church." This was the Vereins-Kirche, built a few months after the arrival of the first colonists and used by all denominations for religious services. The octagon-shaped structure, resembling a coffee mill, was called the "Kaffeemuehle." It was torn down in 1896, and the one standing in Fredericksburg today is a replica of the original drawn by Eastman.

In March Eastman was ordered to the Leona River, where he was to establish and take command of another frontier post, later known as "Fort Inge," now the town of Uvalde. His route was a return to San Antonio, and from there he followed the road west through D'Hanis, Vandenburg, Quihi, and Castroville to the Leona River.

On the return march from Fredericksburg he redated some of his sketches made on the trip out and added six new landscapes.

After March 18 Eastman apparently found less time for the Texas scene. It was a busy time around San Antonio, the hub of all trails west. Since numerous trail blazers and members of the U. S. Topographical Engineers Corps were engaged in expeditions to map and probe the unknown stretches of West Texas, it is likely that Eastman acted as military escort for some of the surveying parties.

From May 7 to July 16 Eastman sketched the Leona and Frio Rivers. His May 18, 1849, view of the encampment on the Leona is doubtless the first one of Fort Inge and of Uvalde. There is another historic scene—where General Wool's army crossed the Frio on his march to Saltillo in 1846.

At least one other sketch made by Eastman while in this area, Fort Lincoln on the Seco River, undated, is in the collection of the Peabody Museum.

Following the last dated and numbered drawing, "Musquite Tree On the Leona, Texas July 16, 1849," are some unrelated and undated sketches of such places as the mouth of the Missouri, Comanche Peak, and Enchanted Rock.

Eastman's notations at times contain inaccuracies in mileages, designations of rivers, and general locations, and the original writing in pencil is traced over in ink, indicating they may have been added at a later date.

The final drawing, captioned by Eastman "Enchanted Rock. 200 miles west by south of Austin, Texas," undated, is an example. The only Enchanted Rock of general knowledge in Texas is the 1,815-foot granite intrusion near Fredericksburg, which would be the logical one for Eastman to sketch. If his mileage is correct, the Rock would be somewhere on the Devil's River in Val Verde County.

Eastman's first Texas tour probably took him farther afield than his Sketchbook or Journal indicates. There is one known Eastman painting of the Texas Staked Plains, formerly in the collection of Eberstadt & Sons, and a drawing of Fort Brown, at the southern tip of the state, in the Peabody Museum.

Eastman's Texas Journal begins August 1, 1849. The writing is extremely small and in places difficult to decipher. It contains no sketches but does include a map, on three separate pages, giving his route with distances, dates, and data from the Leona River to San Antonio and from San Antonio to the Nueces River. He exercised far greater accuracy in map mak-

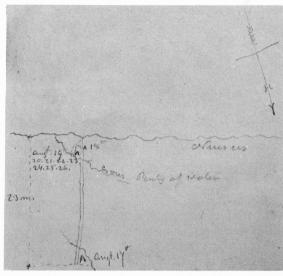

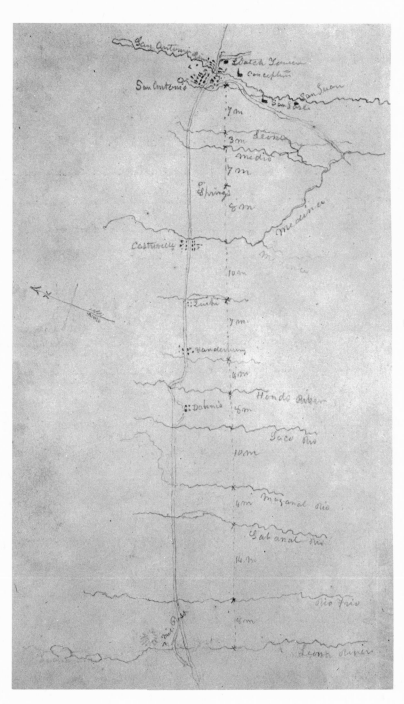

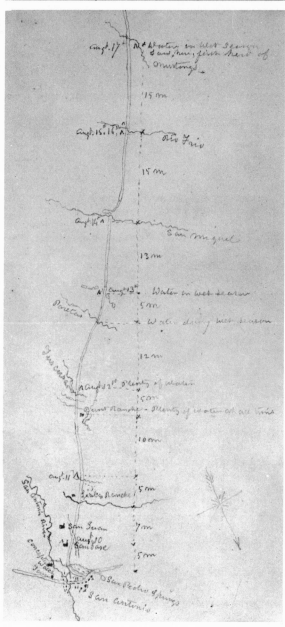

*Map from Captain Eastman's Journal, August 1–14,
1849. (Note the unorthodox directional orientation.)*

ing than in labeling some of his views. It is one of the earliest and most detailed maps of this section of Texas.

The year 1849 was the time of the disastrous cholera epidemic in Texas, when so many settlers and colonists died and westward expeditions were halted by the swift and usually fatal disease.

There was illness in the company from the beginning of the march. When it left San Antonio on August 10 Eastman expected to reach Laredo in nine days. But August 19 found him only as far as the Nueces River, where the map ends with a notation that here the company camped until August 26. The last entry in his Journal was made August 14 when encamped in a "grove of musquites on the San Miguel." No doubt the company was halted by an outbreak of cholera and it is possible that Eastman was a victim.

This reproduction of the Journal follows as closely as possible the original:

Journal of a march from the River Leona Texas to San Antonio (90 miles) thence to Laredo on the Rio Grand (170 miles) in August, 1849—by Capt. S. Eastman, 1st Inf. in command of I Co. 1. Inf.

Augt. 1 1849   Left Leona with Company I 1 Inf. for Laredo, via San Antonio—Encamped on the Rio Frio 7 or 8 miles from Leona—Found the River high—just low enough to enable us to ford with our wagons—Asst Ingineer John Campbell accompany's us as far as San Antonio—

Augt. 2   Broke up camp very early—and got on the march at 4 o'clock—Marched to the Seco 28 miles—Warm day and men much fatigued—arrived at the Seco between one and two oclock. Found Lt Tillinghast, Art, there encamped with 84 Recruits for 1' Inf. Received 16 Recruits—several of them sick—

Augt 3   Broke up camp at 3 o'clock and marched to Quihi 19 miles—met here a party of Haymakers going to Leona to cut hay for Q.M. Dept

Augt 4D   This day marched to Live Oak Spring 8 miles beyond Medina River —in all 18 miles—

Augt 5th   Arrived at San Antonio about 12 oclock—Pitched my camp on the San Pedro 1 miles below Town—Dined with Gen. Brooks to-day—

From 5th to 10th Augt   remained at San Antonio fitting out, to march to Laredo on the Rio Grand—about 170 miles from San Antonio—

Augt 10th   Left San Antonio with 47 soldiers—7 of them sick—8 Wagons—
9 Teamsters 1 Waggon master. 20 days provisions and 10 days forage—expect-
ing to get through in nine days—This day was only a start—went to the Mission
of San Jose five miles and there encamped—Made several sketches during the
day—This old Mission was built about 1800 or a little later—very finely constructed with much sculptur in from around and over the Door—It has been
deserted for years—a few Mexican families now reside around it and in that
portion of the church formerly occupied by the Priests—These old Missions
were constructed by the Jesuits for the purpose of civilizing the Indians—and a
great part of the rough work of building them was done by the Indians—They
are all built of Lime stone—They are now going to ruins—The Mission of Con-
ception is but 2 miles from San Antonio. (below) San Jose 5 miles and San Juan
about 9 miles—all on or very near the San Antonio River—San Jose is the larg-
est and best constructed of the three—The Church of the Alamo situated within
the wall of the Alamo is in San Antonio at the N.E. corner of the town—This is
well built and much ornamented—It is at present in a worst state of ruin than
any of the others—It was in this building that Travis with his small band of
Texian were all massacred by the Mexicans during the Texian revolutions—
David Crockett was one of the numbers   The entire extent of ground covered
by the Alamo must have been about 3 acres—This has been the scene of much
bloodshed—It is built of Lime Stone—At present the whole establishment is
occupied by the U. S. Qr. Mas. Dept—

San Antonio is a Mexican town but rapidly becoming yankeeized—Flat roofs are
giving away to the old fashioned shingled yankee roofs—Most of the houses—
or rather many of them are built of stone cemented with lime—others of Adobie
which are square or rectangular bricks of clay—baked by the sun—These. make
very handsome walls but cannot be very strong—If the outside be not coated
with a thin coat of Lime—the Adobie will be liable to be washed to pieces by
rain—The poorer class of Mexicans build their houses of posts stuck upright in
the earth—leaving an opening for a door and window—A Thatched roof is then
put on, and the crevices stopped up with mud—and behold a Mexican home—
Sometimes a mud chimney is made—no floor excepting the hard clay—one
room only—Generally cook out of doors—To bake they build a semi dome of
mud twenty or thirty feet from the house—when dry they build a fire inside
until sufficiently heated—then put in the bread and stop up the door—San Antonio contains from 5 to 6 thousand inhabitants—formerly, I am told, it contained 15 thousand—It is very compact. very narrow streets—It has no farms—
cottages or retreats around it as is normally found around the towns and cities of
the U. S. When you get to the end of one of the streets, you are at the end of

town—nothing beyond it but a wild prairie over which the Indians roams as free and wild as the ground that he treads—San Antonio is situated on the San Antonio River which is a most beautiful and rapid spring stream—the head of which is but about four miles from the City—The stream runs through town, and the whole city is watered by ditches running from the river and leading through town. On the N.W. side is some very large springs—called San Pedro these springs form quite a large stream that waters the West side—These springs empty into the San Antonio River—The climate being very dry most of the cultivation is done by irrigating the lands—There are two Plazas in San Antonio —the Main Plaza and Mil. Plaza. The front of the Church rests on the former and the rear on the latter—The Mil. Plaza is surrounded by old barrack which are being put in some repair for two Companies of U. S. Infantry that are stationed there—At present this is the main depot for the troops stationed in Texas and the head quarters of the 8th Mil. Dept is here—Before the Americans took possession of this country the Indians were very insolent to the Mexicans and considered them no better than their slaves   A party of Indians would ride into the city stop at a Mexican house, order the owner to hold his horse, and then walk in help themself to what he wants. throw himself on the bed to take a nap and most likely compel the wife or daughter of the one outside holding his horse to go to bed with him—On leaving town they would take any thing they wanted —and never failing of carrying off some female prisoners   These they use as slaves and concubines—Sometimes they take them as wives, but if a squaw becomes jealous she is dispatched without opposition on the part of the men—A case of this kind happened but a short time since as related to me by a Mexican boy that I released after he had been two years prisoner to the Comanches—He says there were four female prisoners in the band that he belonged—Three of these had become pregnant by the husbands of the squaws—which so incited the latter, that they killed the captives and ripped open their bowels—The men never interfering—presuming that they would very shortly replace them by other captive   The Mexicans fear the Indians greatly and the latter hold the former with the utmost contempt—Not so with the Americans—The Indians have been treated to ruffly by the white man that he dread him—he dose not take any liberties with him and will never molest him unless he has clearly the advantage— Since the Americans have ruled at San Antonio no Indians has shown himself within the city—When the Americans first came there and before the Comanche became acquainted with his character—they undertook to treat them as Mexicans but they soon found out it would not do—a few lesson showed them that the white man must be the masters—Much blood was shed—but to the disadvantage of the Indian—Not being able to keep the frontier quite the Americans of San Antonio concluded to have a talk with the Comanches and endeaver to have a peace. About forty of the principals Indians were assembled in a room on the Plaza in San Antonio for that purpose—and about 20 Americans or rather Texians—each armed with a revolver—The Indians armed with Bow and arrows Knives & after talking awhile the chief suddenly raised the war hoop and commenced an attack—After a hard fight nearly every Indian was slain and 6 or 7 Texians—This took place about 1840—Since then no Comanche dare come into San Antonio—

Augt. 11t Started at day-light to continue our march—reached the Medina (7 miles) about nine o·clock—Found the water high—and could just ford it without getting water into our wagons—In starting from this point we took a wrong road and lost several miles by it—After proceeding nearly west for five miles our trail ran out—when we discovered that we had taken the wrong one—by Changing our direction South and going through the woods for about 3 miles we struck the right trail or road—After getting on this road we had some trouble in getting over the next two miles on account of the Quick sands—Frequently we were obliged to unload our wagons and pull them out by hand—We made but 12 miles to-day—On the Medina at the ford is a Ranche or Farm   the only house between San Jose and Laredo—The remainder of the route 160 miles is a perfect wilderness   The soil that we pass over to-day is excellent—and the finest grazing that I ever saw—also plenty of Post Oak good for building—

Augt 12th Started at dawn of day—Road for several miles very sandy—but no quick sands Did not get bogged once to-day. Arrived at Burnt Ranche (10 miles) between 9 and 10 oclock—This is called Burnt Ranche from it once a farm—but was broken up and the house burnt by the Indians—one solitary building alone remains—This farm is situated on a small branch having deep holes in it—So that during a dry season there is always water here—The soil is good and good grazing   The Post Oak timber extends from the Medina to this point—Beyond there is but little timber   Marched about 5 miles further to the Tuscoisa and encamped in a fine grove of oak—Crossed several small branches in these last 5 miles—The water had been up very high, which showed me that it would not have been possible to cross this part of the route when the water is up —but these streams usually run down in 24 to 48 hours—Plenty of snakes about our encampment.

Augt 13 Started at half past three oclock—but found it too dark to see the rattlesnakes in the road—and concluded not to start again until day-light for fear some of the soldiers might get bitten—After marching about 12 miles crossed a small branch called the Perelas—Very little water in it—and probably would be none during a dry season—March 5 miles for then and encamped at a water hole on the road—Very warm day—The only timber we saw to-day was Live Oak and Musquite—Good deal of prairie—good soil—and good grazing—Deer plenty—

Aug. 14th—Broke up camp and got on the march at 4 oclock—rattlesnakes very plenty in the road—killed six and saw a great many to-day—Marched 13 miles and encamped in a grove of musquites on the San Miguel—Plenty of water in this stream in dry weather—Turkies and deer very plenty about our encampment   Early in the morning before day-light heard the snort of a wild horse—The country mostly a rolling prairie interspersed with thin chapperals—Soil does not appear very good—good feed, however, on along the road—The last three miles the road was very gravelly—Killed many rattlesnakes today—

(Note: Eastman's map continues beyond the period covered by the Journal, which ends on August 14, to August 26. From the San Miguel, where the group encamped on August 14, Eastman marched fifteen miles to the Rio Frio, where he encamped August 15 and 16. Fifteen miles farther Eastman's map shows a nameless stream, with this note: "water in wet season; saw here first herd of mustangs." Here he encamped August 17. He crossed a stream [Sous?] twenty-three miles farther on, at which he observed, "Plenty of water." At the Nueces he encamped August 18 through August 26.)

In September Eastman was granted a leave of absence and left Texas for Washington, D. C. Early in 1850 he was given the coveted assignment of illustrating Schoolcraft's report: *Historical and Statistical Information Respecting the History, Condition, and Prospects of the Indian Tribes of the United States.*

The blank pages of his little Texas Journal were used as a scrapbook in which to paste a number of congratulatory letters, newspaper reviews of the report, as well as reviews of books written by his wife.

Among the newspaper clippings is one from the St. Louis *Missouri Republican* of May 23, 1852, signed "H," high in praise of the Schoolcraft-Eastman project. Although he refers in the quotation below to a landscape of the valley of the St. Peter's River from Fort Snelling, H.'s remarks are applicable to all Eastman sketches:

It is given here exactly as it is—nothing added, no effort made to enhance its beauty, but the true reality of the view, as it appeared some five years ago represented;—and now we are told there is a village there! So does scenery change, and man will mar in a few years, with houses, villages and workshops, the glorious views of foliage, and of wild and uncultivated nature, seen from the table land where the Fort is built. We will venture the opinion that in a few years this truthful view will not be recognized as that which it represents; proving how proper it is that views of original scenery should have some permanent place in our annals. We trust the captain will continue these and in some subsequent volume give us views of other and distant scenes, those for instance, connected now with the homes of the Indians in Florida or Texas, and pray let us have, with all its monotony, a good prairie view.

H's entreaty was disregarded. None of the illustrations show Texas views and Indians, and only two have any connection with the general area. One is an inscription from the shoulder-blade of a buffalo "found on the plains in the Comanche country of Texas" and the other an imaginary scene, "Emigrants Attacked by the Comanches."

Eastman finished the illustrations in 1855 and was ordered back to Texas, where until 1856 he was in command of Fort Duncan and Fort Chadbourne. There are no known drawings or paintings of Eastman's second Texas tour of duty.

Eastman, serving throughout the Civil War, was brevetted brigadier general in 1866. After his retirement Congress restored him to active duty to paint oils of Indian scenes and United States forts. He completed twenty-six paintings, now in the Capitol, and was still on this assignment when he died in 1875.

We are most grateful to Mr. Adams for his generosity in permitting the reproduction of the full text and map of the Journal. *The Art of Seth Eastman*, a catalogue of the Smithsonian Institution's 1959–1960 Eastman exhibition written by John Francis McDermott, was frequently consulted in writing this introduction.

Lois Burkhalter

PLATES

NOTE ON THE PLATES

THE SIZE OF THE REPRODUCTIONS IN THIS BOOK IS EXACTLY THE SAME AS THAT OF THE ORIGINAL DRAWINGS. SEVERAL SKETCHES WITH WHICH EASTMAN APPARENTLY WAS DISSATISFIED AND WHICH HE ABANDONED BEFORE COMPLETION HAVE BEEN OMITTED. THE PROCESS USED FOR THE REPRODUCTIONS IS 300-LINE OFFSET.

14 miles above St. Genevieve — 60 miles below St. Louis — looking north.
Oct. 1848

12 miles above St. Genevieve — looking South
Oct. 1848

I

10 miles above St. Genevieve — Looking North.   Oct. 1848

8 miles above St. Genevieve — looking North   Oct. 1848

2

1 mile above St Geneviere - looking North - Oct 1848

Iron Mountain City   looking North   Oct. 1848

Iron Mountain City from 2 miles below —   Looking North   Oct. 1848

4

¼ Mile below St. Louis   Mouth of Kaskaskia River — Looking North — Ille.   Oct. 1848

Kaskaskia — 1 Mile below Kaskaskia River — Looking North M.   Oct. 1848

5

Wrecke 4 miles below Kaskaskia River — looking North

Oct. 1848

2 miles below Kennerson Island — looking North

Oct. 1848

Devils Bake Oven - looking south   Oct. 1848

Devils Bake Oven   looking S. E.   Oct. 1848

7

Grand Tower — Miss. River — looking South

Oct. 1848

Grand Tower — looking S. W.

Oct. 1848

8

Grand Tower — looking West.

Oct. 1848

40 Miles above Cape Giradeau — looking South — 92 miles below St. Louis
Oct. 1848

Opposite preceding

15 *below St Louis*

Hunts Landing – 25 miles above mouth of the Ohio – looking North
Oct 1848

1½ Above S___ ___ville   2 Miles above the Ohio — looking South   Oct 1848

Ohio city   Ohio City — Opposite mouth of Ohio river —   looking West.   140 below St Louis
Oct 1848

Cairo — Mouth of the Ohio — Looking up the River
180 miles below St. Louis   Oct. 1848

Cairo — mouth of the Ohio river
looking West —   Ohio city in the distance —

Mouth of the Ohio - Cairo - looking West 150 below St Louis   Oct. 1848

Cairo - mouth of the Ohio - Ohio city in distance - looking West -   Oct. 1848

13

Miss. Flat Boats at C^t Cairo - Mouth of the Ohio - Oct. 1848

Wharf boat at the mouth of the Ohio —

Oct. 1848

1 Mile above Little Prairie — 105 Miles below mouth of the Ohio — looking West
Oct. 1848

4 Miles below Little Prairie — looking South

Oct. 1848

4 Miles above Needam's Cut off — Old Channel — looking East.
305 below St. Louis

Oct 1848

Foot of Needam's Cut Off   Looking South   Oct 1848

65

4 miles below Ashport, Tenn – looking North
142 miles below mouth of the Ohio

Oct 1848

17

Fulton – Tenn. Looking East – 164 Miles below the Ohio– Oct 1848

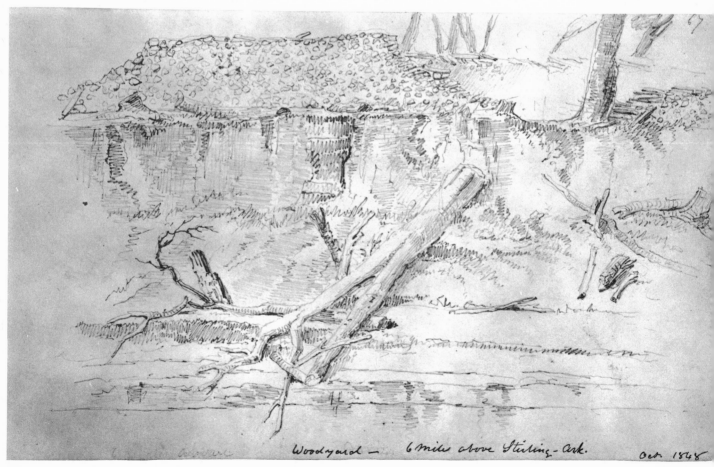

Woodyard – 6 Miles above Sterling – Ark. Oct 1848

18

Woodyard 6 Miles above Sterling

Oct. 1848

Sterling. Ark. At the mouth of St. Francis River - 814 miles below the Ohio - looking West
461 below St Louis

Oct. 1848

ale.   Sterling – looking North
                                                Oct. 1848

1 Mile below Sterling – looking North – Ark. and Miss.   ale Oct. 1848

4 Miles below Sterling – looking North   Oct. 1848

4 Miles above Helena – looking North   Oct. 1848

324 miles below the Ohio – Helena – Ark – Looking South – Oct. 1848

Helena. Ark. looking N. W. Oct. 1848

Cottage on the Miss. in Ark. below Helena   Oct. 1848

Cotton Plantation. Ark. looking West   Oct. 1848

Cotton Plantation. Ark. 60 miles above Vicksburg. looking North Oct. 1848

Buena Vista landing - 55 miles above Vicksburg - looking N E Oct. 1848

24

10 miles below Milliken's Bend. or 5 miles above Yazoo River. looking North
7485 below St Louis

Oct 1848.

Mouth of Yazoo River. Miss. miles below the Ohio

Oct 1848

82

Vicksburg – looking looking North. 632 miles below the Ohio
Oct. 1848

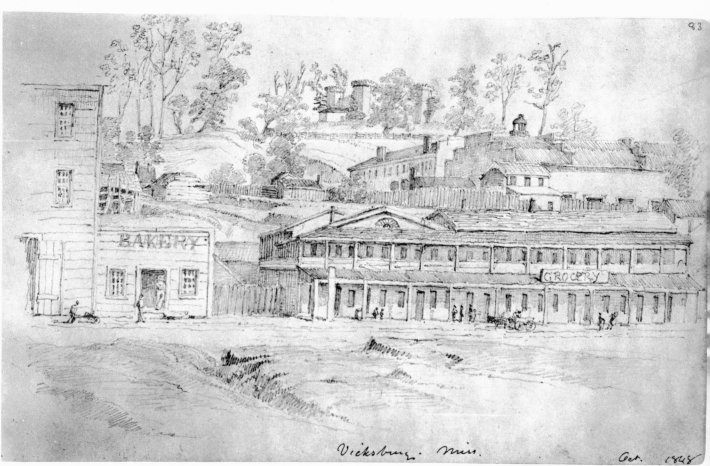

83

BAKERY

GROCERY

Vicksburg. Miss.
Oct. 1848

Vicksburg. Looking South   Oct. 1848

3 miles below Natchez. 739 miles below The Ohio
919 below St Louis   Oct. 1848

Ellis Bluff. 14 Miles below Natchez. looking South
Oct. 1848

Ellis Bluff - looking N. E.

Oct. 1848

28

Loftus Heights on Fort Adams. 793 miles below the Ohio — looking North   Oct 1848

11 miles above Bayou Sara - looking S.W. 855 miles below the Ohio.

Oct. 1848

1030 miles below the Ohio

89

Sugar Plantation. 10 miles above New-Orleans. looking West. Oct. 1848

Sugar Plantation just above N. O. looking North

Oct. 1848

1040 miles below the Ohio — 2044 from Pittsburg — 1212 from St. Louis
105 from the Balize — 17 from Fort St. Leon — 75 from Fort St. Phillips 71
1944 from Fort Snelling

West

New-Orleans from the Barracks- looking West

Oct. 1848

New Orleans from the Tower at the Barracks
Oct 1848

Pilots Houses at the Mouth of the Miss.

October 31

32

Pilot Houses. S. W. Pass. Mouth of the Miss

Oct. 31. 1848

looking South

Mouth of the Miss. S. W. Pass. looking South

Oct. 31. 1848

Mouth of the Miss. looking South from the Deck of a Steam boat

Oct 31. 1848

Mouth of the Miss. looking North. S.W. Pass.

Nov. 1. 1848

mouth of the Miss. S.W. Pass. — looking S.

Oct. 31. 1848

Entrance to Matagorda Bay. Texas — Pilot Houses.

Nov. 1848

36

Entrance to Matagorda Bay. Texas.   looking out to sea.
Point
Nov. 1848

Indian Point. Texas. 12 miles below Port Lavacca
Nov. 12. 1848

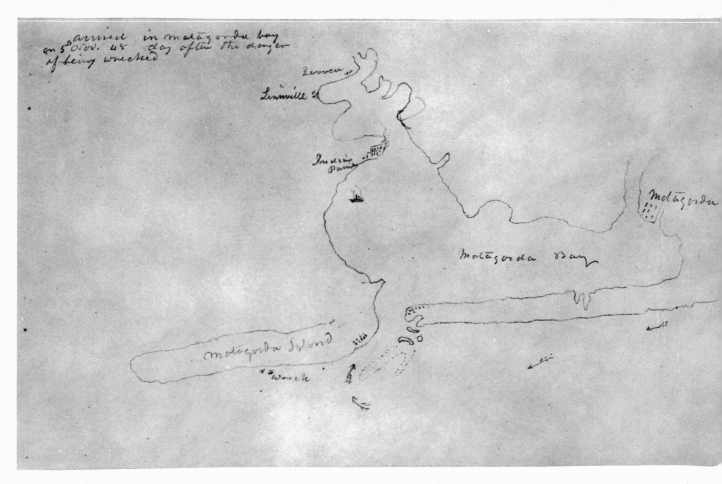

arrived in matagorda bay
on 5ᵗʰ Nov. 48 day after the danger
of being wrecked

Levver

Linnville

Indian
Point

Matagorda

Matagorda Bay

Matagorda Island

Wreck

102

Indian Point. looking N. W.

Nov. 1848

38

Post Oak.   Texas. Nov. 15th 1848

Post Oak

Texas.   Nov. 16th 1848

Post Oaks.
4 miles from Seguin. Texas.

Nov. 18. 1848

Live Oaks.
4 miles from Seguin. Texas

Nov. 18. 1848

Seguin, Texas — looking North   Nov. 19th. 1848

Live Oaks.

At Seguin. Texas. looking South   Nov. 19. 1848

Live Oaks
2 Miles from Seguin. Texas   Nov. 19. 1848

Part Oak   musquite tree 110

13 Miles from Seguin. Texas.   evening of 19° Nov. 1848

10 miles from San Antonio. Texas. evening of Nov. 20ᵗʰ 1848

Front View of the Mission Chapel of San Jose. 5 miles from San Antonio. Texas.   Nov. 1848

The Alamo. at San Antonio. Texas.

Nov. 22 1848

Mexican house in San Antonio. Texas. Part of the Alamo.

Nov 22 1848

44

Front view of the Alamo. Texas

Nov. 1848

San Antonio. Texas. from near the old Watch Tower. looking north

Nov 22 1848

Chapel within the Alemo at San Antonio. Texas— East Side

Nov. 1848

Old Mexican Lookout or Watch Tower at San Antonio. Texas. 2 miles from the Alemo.

Nov 22 1848

46

Mission Chapel of San Jose 5 miles from San Antonio. Texas   Nov. 24" 1846

20 Miles North of San Antonio. Texas Dec 2 1848 looking South

47

30 miles North of San Antonio. Texas — looking East 2ᵈ Dec 1848

Camp at Sebina Creek. 33 miles North of San Antonio Dec 2 1848

Sabina creek

34 Miles North of San Antonio. Texas   looking South   Dec 3 1848

46 miles North of San Antonio. Texas. —   Sister Creek   Encamped Dec 3 1848

49 miles North of San Antonio.   Comanche country looking South   Dec 4th 1848

Comanche country — 50 miles North of San Antonio, Texas — looking South   Dec 4th 1848

Camp Houston – near Fredericksburg – Texas –   65 miles north of San Antonio   Dec 30ᵗʰ 1848

Live Oak near Fredericksburg. Texas   January 23 1849

51

January 24th 1849.   Dutch Church at Fredericksburg, Texas - 70 Miles North of San Antonio

Live Oaks at Fredericksburg, Texas -

January 24th 1849

132

Dutch house in Fredericksburg Texas   January 25th 184.

133

Dutch House in Fredericksburg Texas   January 26 184.

53

Live Oak near Fredericksburg – Texas –

Jany 31^t 1849

Dutch House at Fredericksburg. Texas.

Jany 26th 1849

54

Dutch House in Fredericksburg, Texas. January 27, 1849

Dutch House in Fredericksburg Texas. residence of the Parson. January 28 1849

Dutch House in Fredericksburg – Texas   Janny 29 1849.

Live Oak near Fredericksburg – Texas   Janny 31 1849

Distant view of Fredericksburg — valley of the Pendanalis   Texas   Feb. 1. 1849.

Dutch House in Fredericksburg — Texas —   Feb. 12th 1849

view from Fredericksburg. Texas. Feb. 24. 1849

From Sabina Creek looking West. Texas.   March 11th 1849

8 miles south of Sabina Creek. Texas
looking east

March 11th 1849

C. Meusebach

24 miles from San Antonio - Texas - looking south - 6 miles north of Braunfels
March 13th 1849

146

30 Miles north of San Antonio. Texas   Encampment March 11th 1849. looking [...]

147

Texas.   2 Miles from Baron Meusebach [...]   March 13

1849

60

At Encampment on the Salado 12 miles north of San Antonio Texas   March 13th 1849
Clio pupped   146

Steeple too more mirror   147

Church in the Plaza at San Antonio Texas   1849   Mar 1849

61

From the Leona River – Texas – May 7th 1849

Encampment on the Leona – Texas – 80 miles west of San Antonio May 13th 1849

Rocks on the Leona. Texas. May. 15th 1849

90 miles West of San Antonio. Encampment on the Leona from the Mound. Texas. May 18 1849

Leona River - Texas -   May 25th 1849

Leona River - Texas -   May 25th /49

Rio Frio - at the crossing of Wool road - Texas   Rio Frio   May 26. 1849

Live Oak - on the Leona - Texas   July 13th 1849

Elm trees   On the Leona — Texas —   July 15th 1849

Mus quite Tree   on the Leona — Texas   July 16th 1849

66

mesquite tree   on the Leona - Texas   July 16. 1849

mouth of the Missouri

Comanche Peak – 15 miles N. E. of San Antonio – Texas

Enchanted Rock. 200 miles west by south of Austin – Texas

68